Anwar Sadat: The Life and Legacy of the Egyptian President

By Charles River Editors

About Charles River Editors

Charles River Editors provides superior editing and original writing services across the digital publishing industry, with the expertise to create digital content for publishers across a vast range of subject matter. In addition to providing original digital content for third party publishers, we also republish civilization's greatest literary works, bringing them to new generations of readers via ebooks.

Sign up here to receive updates about free books as we publish them, and visit Our Kindle Author Page to browse today's free promotions and our most recently published Kindle titles.

Introduction

Anwar Sadat (1981)

On a beautiful sunny day in March 1979, as thousands of Egyptians awaited in anticipation, a plane landed in Cairo. Moments later, Egyptian President Anwar Sadat stepped out, welcomed by thunderous cheers from an overjoyed crowd. He had just returned to his country from Washington D.C., where five days earlier he had signed a historic treaty with Israeli Prime Minister Menachem Begin and U.S. President Jimmy Carter, bringing an end to three decades of war and hostilities between Israelis and Egyptians. Few moments in the history of this region were as momentous and poignant as the signing of this treaty, the first between Israel and any Arab country, and Egyptians across the country hailed Sadat as their hero and expressed pride in their leader, the bringer of peace.

Egypt had good reason to celebrate the treaty. Since 1948, the country joined other Arab states and went to war with Israel on four occasions: the 1948 Arab-Israeli War, the 1956 War, the 1967 Six-Day War, and the 1973 Yom Kippur War. All were ultimately unsuccessful in fully defeating Israel, and Egypt, of all the Arab states, experienced the heaviest losses, both in human casualties and financially. It was Sadat's deep-seated resolve and the will of the Egyptian people that forged the path to the unprecedented normalization of relations between Israel and an Arab country.

Pride in and respect for Anwar Sadat was not limited to his people either, as much of the world touted Sadat as a great world leader and peacemaker. Together with Begin, Sadat was awarded the Nobel Peace Prize in 1978 for their efforts in negotiating the peace treaty. Sadat was applauded by leaders of democratic nations across the world, and he opened up a new chapter of Egyptian foreign relations, establishing the country as a modernized and stable power in the historically tumultuous Middle East.

As a result of his efforts, Sadat, in 1981, at the age of 62, was hailed as the "Architect of a new Mideast" and ranked as a dominant and often-dazzling figure on the stage of international politics. Yet only ten years earlier, he was being mocked by world leaders as a clown. And in 1970, when Sadat was Egypt's vice-president, his predecessor as president mocked him as "old Goha," a legendary victim, or "fall guy," in Egyptian folklore. He once said that "Sadat's greatest ambition is to own a big automobile and have the government pay for the gasoline."

A significant figure in his own right, Sadat was determined to set himself apart, but he was often compared to his good friend and predecessor Gamal Abdel Nasser. However, this was a man who was passionate about more than just peace; he fought diligently for the stabilization and growth of his country, for the implementation of a wide-reaching open-door economic policy, and for the strengthening of the Egyptian culture, spirit, and nation. Though he was often seen as the protégé of Nasser, and he certainly was, he proved to be much more than that as he made a significant effort to emerge from his predecessor's shadow.

As with many historic moments that inspired significant change, not everyone was supportive of Sadat's peace efforts. Only two years after the signing of the Egyptian-Israeli Peace Treaty, President Sadat was assassinated by members of an Islamic fundamentalist group, the Egyptian Islamic Jihad, in October 1981. As a president who succeeded the revolutionary Gamal Abdel Nasser and was succeeded by the long-reigning Hosni Mubarak, Sadat and his legacy are often overshadowed by the forceful prowess and authoritative legacies of Nasser and Mubarak, his presidency reduced to the peace treaty and the subsequent Nobel Prize he received. In fact, Sadat appeared to have suffered from a misrepresented image for much of his military and political career. Historian George Sullivan wrote in Sadat: The Man Who Changed Mid-East History:

Over three decades since the death of Sadat, the Middle East and the world still wonder, discuss, and debate his legacy. Recent events like the 2011 Arab Spring, the toppling of what was long thought to be an indomitable Mubarak regime, the rise and fall of the Islamist Muslim Brotherhood, and turbulent relations with Israel have raised more questions and controversy about Sadat's vision for his country and the region. The Egypt that Sadat envisioned and worked so hard for has yet to become a reality, and in fact, it often appears to never be within reach. A Washington Institute tribute to Sadat on the twentieth anniversary of his death put it quite aptly – that there exists among historians and scholars a "relative unease…in finding a place for Sadat" in Egyptian history "The fact is that there remains a tension about Sadat, an inability to explain a man who appeared equally comfortable with peasants and presidents, a man who seemed at home with a feisty international press corps yet who imprisoned thousands of his domestic political opponents."

Though the significance and true impact of Sadat and his legacy may be difficult to define, it can certainly be said that Sadat inhabits a unique place in Egyptian history. Compared to Nasser's chaotic and rallying rule and Mubarak's oppressive reign, Sadat's presidency was marked with stability, reform, and above all, a yearning for peace. The peace efforts that Sadat undertook permanently changed the political, economic, and social character of Egypt, and though he was praised as a hero by many yet cursed as traitor by some, a majority of Egyptians fell in the former group, or at least acknowledged Sadat's courage and hard work.

Anwar Sadat: The Life and Legacy of the Egyptian President chronicles the life and legacy of one of Egypt's most famous presidents. Along with pictures of important people, places, and events, you will learn about Sadat like never before, in no time at all.

Anwar Sadat: The Life and Legacy of the Egyptian President

About Charles River Editors

Introduction

   Chapter 1: The Early Life and Revolutionary Activities of Sadat

   Chapter 2: President Gamal Abdel Nasser

   Chapter 3: Sadat's Presidency

   Chapter 4: The Legacy of Anwar Sadat

   Bibliography

Chapter 1: The Early Life and Revolutionary Activities of Sadat

On December 25, 1918, Anwar Sadat was born in Mit Abul-Kum, a small village approximately 60 miles from Cairo. Sadat was one of 13 children; his mother was Sudanese Nubian, and his father, an Egyptian Nubian who worked as a clerk as a military hospital clerk, was an avid supporter of Turkey's revolutionary leader, Mustafa Kemal Ataturk. Throughout his childhood and even during his presidency, Sadat suffered greatly for his skin color, which was darker than that of average Egyptians because of his African blood; he faced frequent criticisms of not looking "Egyptian enough" and was ridiculed for years as "Nasser's black poodle."[1]

Ataturk

It has been written that four figures deeply impacted young Anwar Sadat and continued to affect him throughout his life. The first was a man who appeared in a story his grandmother told him, the "hero of Denshway" – a man named Zahran, from a small village like his own, who was hanged for participating in a violent riot that had resulted in the death of a British officer.[2] As he walked to the scaffolds to his death, it was said that Zahran proudly proclaimed, "I am dying to free Egypt." As his daughter Camelia Anwar Sadat wrote, "Throughout his life, my father saw

---
[1] Sunni M. Khalid, "The Root: Race and Racism Divide Egypt," *NPR*, February 7, 2011. http://www.npr.org/2011/02/07/133362448/the-root-egypts-race-problem.
[2] Sullivan, *Sadat: The Man Who Changed Mid-East History*, 17.

himself as Zahran, as a true patriot."[3]

The second man who inspired Sadat was Mustafa Kemal Ataturk, the same man his father greatly admired. Ataturk was an inspirational figure for many during the 1920s; he was the epitome of the modern anti-colonialist, who had created the state of Turkey by ousting all foreign colonial influence and orchestrating the downfall of the long-reigning Ottoman Empire. The secular and liberal reforms that Ataturk engineered in the previously Islamic empire were unprecedented during these times, and Sadat admired the man greatly for his courage to stand up to greater powers and make his vision a reality.[4]

The third man who impacted young Sadat was Mohandas Gandhi, the world-renowned figurehead for peace and nonviolence. When Gandhi toured Egypt in 1932, Sadat was inspired by his speeches on combating injustice through nonviolent means and carefully pored over Gandhi's writings on peaceful resistance against the British occupation of India – perhaps an early indicator of his peace efforts with Israel. It is said that Sadat admired Gandhi to such an extent that he stopped wearing clothing and instead took to covering himself with an apron, in an attempt to emulate Gandhi's austere form of dress. Because Gandhi was rumored to spin his own thread for his clothing, young Sadat also made a spindle and attempted to spin his own thread.[5]

---

[3] Camelia Anwar Sadat and Ahmed Maher El-Sayed, "Anwar Sadat and His Vision," in *Sadat and His Legacy*, ed. Jon B. Alterman (Washington DC: Washington Institute for Near East Policy, 1998), 3.
[4] "Anwar Al-Sadat," accessed June 2, 2014,
https://web.archive.org/web/20090125000520/http://ibiblio.org/sullivan/bios/Sadat-bio.html.
[5] Heather Lehr Wagner, *Anwar Sadat and Menachem Begin: Negotiating Peace in the Middle East* (New York: Infobase Publishing, 2007), 15.

Gandhi

Finally, the fourth man who inspired Sadat was Adolf Hitler, whom Sadat admired for his charisma, his leadership, and his ability to rebuild a shattered nation. In Sadat's eyes, Hitler's fervently anti-colonialist stance made him a potential rival to British imperialism, and anyone challenging the British was a hero to Sadat.[6] Though Hitler's anti-colonialist methods completely opposed those of Mohandas Gandhi, Hitler demonstrated military prowess and skills that surprised and affected the entire world. Sadat became engrossed by Hitler, his Nazi German army, and their ability to quickly become a severe and strategic threat to big foreign powers, notably Britain and the U.S..[7]

---

[6] "Anwar Al-Sadat," accessed June 2, 2014,
https://web.archive.org/web/20090125000520/http://ibiblio.org/sullivan/bios/Sadat-bio.html.

Though after four decades as a British protectorate, Egypt had gained independence from Britain in February 1922, it was a nominal freedom; the country was still very much under the control of the British, and Britain continued to maintain a strong military presence in Egypt. Though it was renamed in its post-independence days as the Kingdom of Egypt, the country's sovereignty was nonetheless subject to severe restrictions imposed by its former occupiers; the kingdom continued to experience significant British influence and intervention in its political, fiscal, administrative, and governmental affairs. Additionally, Britain retained its control of the Suez Canal – a key waterway for trade and transportation, and a primary interest of Britain and other European powers. The Egyptian people were disheartened and frustrated by this "independence," which was in truth just a continuation of the status quo under a different name.

In the early 1920s, the nationalist Wafd party gained popularity, quickly becoming one of the most influential and active political parties in post-independence Egypt. Fervently opposing European interference in Egyptian affairs and calling for the immediate termination of British occupation, the Wafd party represented the voice and anger of many Egyptians tired of their country being utilized for the benefit of foreign powers, and at the expense of the domestic population. Uprisings, riots, and rallies were organized by the Wafd, and the party steadily grew to become Egypt's preeminent political party. In the 1924 parliamentary elections, the Wafd won an astonishing 179 of 211 parliamentary seats, and in 1936, the Wafd again won 89% of the vote and 157 of 211 seats.[8]

It was in this nationalistic environment that Anwar Sadat was born and raised. Though as a poor peasant boy, he had little direct contact with the politics of Egypt as a child, the spirit of nationalism and anti-colonialism permeated throughout the country. As with many leaders and seminal figures, it is only by examining the historical context in which they lived that their legacies can be assessed. Sadat's vision for Egypt, forged during his early childhood and carried throughout his ascendancy to vice presidency and presidency, was not borne out of meticulous planning or academics, but out of plain passion and visceral nationalism – something he shared with millions of other ordinary Egyptians.

It can be said that the development of Anwar Sadat's political views and his ascendance into the realm of Egyptian politics began with his military service. It was in the military that Sadat escaped the poverty of his youth, received education and practical training, learned his strengths and weaknesses, and most importantly, met and engaged with fellow officers with whom he could exchange thoughts and ideas.

Previously, entrance into Egypt's royal military academy was an option reserved solely for Egypt's elite and middle class. However, in 1936, the ruling Wafd party that had come into

---

[7] Anwar Sadat's admiration for Adolf Hitler was the only one of the four that did not last, at least publically. After he became president, Sadat made statements indicating his hostility for Hitler, and he used the term "Nazi" as a pejorative, usually directing it against Israel.

[8] Helen Chapin Metz, ed. *Egypt: A Country Study* (Washington: GPO for the Library of Congress, 1990), 49-50.

power opened up the doors of the military academy in an effort to ride the anti-colonialism wave that was sweeping the country and develop a military filled with nationalistic, politically active youth who would pave the path toward complete Egyptian independence. The results were as intended – the opening up of the military academy brought together the very people who were most eager for a change in the status quo – young men of the lower classes with no stake in preserving the existing power structures, including Sadat, who was among the academy's first students.

Sadat was only 18 years old when the military academy opened its doors in 1936. He overcame the challenges he encountered in submitting his application, and he entered the academy the same year, in 1936. His two-year training covered diverse subjects and topics he barely had the opportunity to extensively study while in school; in addition to learning traditional subjects such as math and science, the cadets also studied Egyptian history, world history, and the tactics and strategies used in famous military battles. It was in the academy that Sadat learned and read more extensively about great military leaders, such as Mustafa Kemal Ataturk, and took up studying the Turkish revolution.[9]

It is no surprise then that when he graduated from the military academy in 1938, armed with an arsenal of knowledge and training, Sadat was even more inspired to seek out ways to resist the British occupation of Egypt. It is interesting to note that despite Sadat's long-holding admiration for Mohandas Gandhi, neither nonviolent revolution nor peaceful resistance was on his mind at this time. His boyhood days of emulating Gandhi and his ways were seemingly gone, replaced by a hardness and raw determination that his military studies had instilled. Sadat became convinced that the only way to liberate Egypt from British occupation and colonialism was not through diplomacy, but through forceful means. Though the military academy had a large role in shaping his newfound beliefs, another part of Sadat's change of mind came from getting a glimpse into how the Egyptian government worked. He realized how weak the government was, its self-interested officials all under the thumb of the British. Sadat grew convinced that the only way for true independence was the complete overhaul of the current regime – an armed revolution.[10]

Upon his graduation, Sadat began his military training and also married; he was eventually posted to a government base in Manqabad, a small town in upper Egypt.[11] Though Sadat was disheartened by his appointment to such a remote place, as he believed any change and revolution must start in the capital, he quickly shifted his focus to training and teaching those around him about the state of Egypt's subservience to Britain and the armed revolution he planned to bring about. He therefore held many meetings with his fellow officers, sometimes

---

[9] Wagner, *Anwar Sadat and Menachem Begin: Negotiating Peace in the Middle East*, 15-20.
[10] Magdalena Alagna, *Anwar Sadat* (New York: Rosen Publishing Group, 2004), 26.
[11] "Mohamed Anwar El-Sadat," *State Information Service Your Gateway to Egypt*, July 20, 2009, http://www.sis.gov.eg/En/Templates/Articles/tmpArticles.aspx?ArtID=1665#.U921uvmSy18.

speaking with them privately, at other times lecturing them in a group. Sadat's room at the Manqabad base came to be known as "The National Assembly," as the frequency and number of soldiers participating in these meetings grew.[12]

It was at one of these "National Assembly" meetings that Sadat first met Gamal Abdel Nasser, the man who would later become the architect of the free Egypt Sadat envisioned, and who would so greatly affect Sadat's life and impact the history of Egypt. Sadat later recalled his first meeting with Nasser: "My impression was that he was a serious-minded youth who did not share his fellows' interest in jesting, nor would he allow anyone to be frivolous with him as this, he felt, would be an affront to his dignity. Most of my colleagues therefore kept their distance and even refrained from talking to him for fear of being misunderstood."[13] Still, Sadat felt no reservations against the man who was to later become his president. He quickly befriended Nasser, who agreed with Sadat that a change was necessary to restore the pride of the Egyptian people and liberate the country. This marked the start of a long and fruitful friendship; little did either of them know that their friendship would shape the future of the country for decades to come.

Nasser, Sadat, Ali Sabri, and Vice President Hussein el-Shafei in 1968

In 1939, Sadat and Nasser founded a revolutionary nationalist group they called the Free

---

[12] Raymond Carroll, *Anwar Sadat* (New York: F. Watts, 1982), 18.
[13] Joseph Finklestone, *Anwar Sadat: Visionary Who Dared* (London: Frank Cass Publishers, 1996), 11.

Officers Organization. The group was intended to be a secretive organization composed of junior officers in the Egyptian army – a network of nationalist soldiers, all aiming to utilize their positions in the military to orchestrate the toppling of the Egyptian government and the complete ouster of all foreign influence from Egypt. Later, Sadat recounted the six principles the group was formed to uphold: "the elimination of imperialism, the destruction of feudalism, the establishment of social justice, the formation of a strong Egyptian Army, the creation of sound democratic life, and the liberation of the government from the control of capitalists."[14]

In 1939, to Sadat's delight, he was transferred out of the Manqabad base and stationed in Maadi, located outside Cairo. There, he was subsequently appointed to the newly-formed Signal Corps, and with his military career secured, Sadat and several of his fellow officers continued their clandestine meetings and discussions.[15] Encouraged by British defeats to the Germans in 1939 and 1940, Sadat enthusiastically increased his political activity, holding meeting in the officers' mess and cafes, approaching more senior officers and furtively planting seeds of an armed revolution in their minds, and organizing the loosely knit Free Officers Organization into a more cohesive underground network.

In 1941, Sadat was again relocated, this time to Marsa Matruh on the Mediterranean. Here, Sadat continued his efforts to devise a plan for an immediate armed revolution; he was in a rush, particularly because the British were growing weak and continuing to experience defeat after defeat in Asia, Europe, and North Africa. When the British ordered all Egyptian units to withdraw from Marsa Matruh, Sadat chose to stand his ground, believing this to be the perfect opportunity for revolution. He proposed to his fellow officers that all of their units should regroup and march into Cairo while the security was still unstable and seize the government by force. Yet, he was met only with great disappointment when he waited at the meeting location and discovered that not a single unit was there to meet him. Sadat's first attempt at revolution ended in utter failure; fortunately or unfortunately, neither the Egyptian government nor the British ever knew that it had taken place.[16]

Though hostile sentiment against the British ran high during these times, and anything that set the British back was seen as a victory among much of the population in Egypt, there was also a realization that if the British were to lose the world war, it would not necessarily grant Egypt freedom; the speculation was that Egypt would simply be passed on to another foreign power, possibly Italy. Sadat and his fellow Free Officers were concerned about this possibility, prompting them to draft a "treaty" that offered to recruit and train an army of committed Egyptian officers to fight alongside Axis powers against the British in exchange for total Egyptian independence after the war. In an attempt to get this proposal to the attention of the Germans, Sadat sought out two German agents in Cairo, who were later arrested and interrogated

---

[14] Ibid., 12.
[15] Alagna, *Anwar Sadat*, 30.
[16] Carroll, *Anwar Sadat*, 20.

by British intelligence. Sadat was swiftly implicated and subsequently detained by British and Egyptian authorities; he was stripped of his rank and imprisoned. Sadat was imprisoned at a series of detention centers over the next two years, and though he was understandably discouraged by this setback in his plans, he was not quick to give up. In order to use his time in prison as constructively as he could, Sadat read extensively and studied English and German.[17]

By the end of 1942, Nasser had established himself as leader of the Free Officers. Throughout the next few years, Nasser strengthened the organization while Sadat continued under detention. When martial law was finally lifted at the end of World War II in 1945, under which Sadat had been detained, he was released and subsequently reinstated in the armed forces as captain, the same rank he had prior to his arrest and detention. It was upon his release that Sadat learned from Nasser just how much the Free Officers Organization had changed and grown, not just in membership, but in a different way than Sadat had imagined. In his autobiography, Sadat recalled that "Nasser's leadership of the Free Officers' Association differed from mine. He created secret units in the army, each unknown to each other. The numbers increased daily until the organization included members in the entire armed forces, especially sensitive departments such as the army administration."[18] Thus, the organization had developed into a cell system modeled after underground Marxist groups; the membership in each cell was kept secret and unknown outside the cell itself, and members of each cell had no knowledge of the identity of the leadership.

Perhaps it was because the changes he saw in the movement he had helped establish with Nasser were so immense that Sadat avoided rejoining it. After his release from prison, instead of returning to the Free Officers Organization, Sadat began developing his own independent revolutionary activities. After years of detention, the freedom to execute all the thoughts and plots that had festered in his mind during imprisonment overwhelmed him; he later recalled that he "started to form a secret organization, feeling that personal liberty could hardly be real until [his] entire homeland had been liberated."[19] Sadat teamed up with several other revolutionaries to plot assassinations of Egyptian politicians whom they perceived as being cooperative with the British – one of these plots included a grenade attack on Mustafa el-Nahas, head of the Waft party that Sadat and his co-plotters viewed as traitors for obediently operating within the British-imposed political system. Though most of these assassination plots were not executed or failed, one did succeed; on January 6, 1946, a young member of Sadat's group shot dead Amin Osman Pasha, a pro-British politician and prominent member of the aristocracy.[20]

---

[17] Ibid., 21-22.
[18] Anwar El-Sadat, *Those I Have Known* (New York: Continuum, 1984), 77-78.
[19] Ibid., 23.
[20] Ibid., 24.

Mustafa el-Nahas

The assassination of Pasha received widespread media attention, and much of the populace cheered for the death of a staunch supporter of the British occupation. After his first step into terrorism, Sadat became even more convinced that violent means were not only effective, but also the only way to achieve real political change. However, police were able to quickly apprehend the assassin, who gave up Sadat, leading to his second arrest. Sadat recalled of his subsequent solitary confinement at Cairo Central Prison: "It was four o'clock in the afternoon when I found myself inside Cell 54…there was no bed, no small table, no chair and no simple lamp. It was completely bare—apart from the palm-fibre mat on the macadamized floor, hardly big enough for a man to sleep on, and an unbelievably dirty blanket. You can't imagine how filthy that thing was. In the winter water oozed from the cell walls day and night, and in the summer huge armies of bugs marched up and down…I lived for a whole eighteen months in that hole, unable to read or write or listen to the radio. I was denied everything, even a single lamp."[21]

As is true for many who become involved in politically-motivated violence and terrorism, imprisonment only led to Sadat's increased radicalization, feeding his anger. Solitary confinement gave Sadat much time for reflection, self-examination, and planning for a future revolution. After two and a half years in prison, Sadat was acquitted and released.

---

[21] Ibid., 24.

It was 1950, and Sadat had already wasted several precious years. He knew he could afford to make no more mistakes, and so this time after his release, he rejoined the Free Officers Organization, which was the most organized opposition movement in his mind. Even after eight years of imprisonment and being away from the Free Officers, Sadat was welcomed by Nasser and subsequently chosen as one of the members of Nasser's newly established Constituent Committee within the Free Officers Organization – a body composed of those leading officers who were most trusted by and loyal to Nasser. Sadat, though initially not a leading member, quickly rose up the ranks and gained influence in the Constituent Committee. As Sadat wrote himself, he added to the Committee "another element, that of intelligence…it was not difficult for Nasser to realize that he could depend on me, and that his act of loyalty in selecting me would make me, in turn, loyal to him for life."[22]

Indeed, Sadat did bring a new perspective and views to the Committee composed mainly of shadowy self-purported revolutionaries, radical nationalist, Marxists, and socialists – all with goals and intentions that were masked to Sadat. For example, Sadat was able to convince Nasser not to pursue his initial plans for political assassinations, bringing up his own failures as proof that individual acts of violence would never bring about a large-scale revolution. Instead, he argued that efforts must be placed on instigating a military coup, thus dissuading Nasser and the Free Officer Organization from pursuing terrorism as a tactic.[23]

The Egyptian Revolution of 1952, also known as the 23 July Revolution, transpired in an era when anti-monarchy, anti-colonialism, and anti-British sentiment were at an all-time high all across Egypt, giving Sadat, Nasser, and the Free Officers enough impetus to implement their dream of a full-scale revolution. Even without the provocation of the Free Officers Organization, in early 1952, spontaneous riots broke out on the streets – evidence of the highly charged and tense environment in which the revolution eventually took place.

Thirty-three-year-old Sadat, then posted in al-Arish in the Sinai Peninsula, received an urgent message from Nasser on July 21, telling him to come to Cairo, as the revolution was starting. When Sadat got to Cairo, he found that the revolution indeed had already begun; the rebels had already stormed numerous military bases and arrested top military officers. Following Nasser's orders, Sadat took control of the telephones and served as the communications officer, contacting rebel leaders in the Sinai, the Western Desert, Alexandria, and other major cities in Egypt and coordinating their offensive.

Two days later, on July 23, Sadat was instructed by Nasser to seize control of the Cairo radio station and broadcast an official proclamation to the people announcing the coup. He did, and the reaction on the streets was mixed; though many were overjoyed by the toppling of the British-controlled government and the fall of the foreign powers' puppet, King Farouk, they did not

---

[22] El-Sadat, *Those I Have Known*, 79.
[23] Carroll, *Anwar Sadat*, 31.

know what was to replace the old system of rule, and whether it would be any different or beneficial to the people of Egypt. As Sadat himself described, there was a "festive silence" in the streets of Egypt's cities that day.[24]

The next job Sadat was tasked with was to communicate to King Farouk the terms of the ultimatum the rebels were presenting – either the king could leave Egypt by six o'clock that evening, or he could suffer the consequences deemed fit by the rebels. Unsurprisingly, King Farouk chose a swift departure; on July 26, 1952, the last king of Egypt left his country for exile in Italy.[25] The revolution that Sadat, Nasser, and their fellow fighters had all dreamed about had finally become a reality.

King Farouk I

Thus, the revolution unfolded surprisingly quickly, with the abdication and exile of King Farouk achieved in a mere few days. Though the overthrow of the king had been the initial and

---
[24] Ibid., 33.
[25] Amina Elbendary, "The Long Revolution," *Al-Ahram*, July 18, 2002, http://weekly.ahram.org.eg/2002/595/sc2.htm.

primary goal of the revolution, the Free Officers quickly moved to achieve further political goals, including abolishing the constitutional monarchy and the high status of the Egyptian aristocracy, establishing the Republic of Egypt, ending the British occupation of Egypt, and securing the independence of neighboring Sudan, which had also been under the control of the British. The new revolutionary government adopted a staunchly nationalist agenda, ushering in the spread of what came to be known as Arab nationalism, or Nasserism – an ideological movement comprising components of anti-imperialism, pan-Arabism, nationalism, and Arab socialism. The results of the revolution were not constrained to the borders of Egypt; Nasserism was exported to other countries as "a psychological phenomenon shared by an entire Arab generation." Nasserism was less an ideological movement the likes of Marxism or Leninism, and more an "attitude of mind" that had appealed to and spread across other Arab countries, giving them a feeling of confidence themselves, largely counterbalancing the psychological shock of the loss of Palestine in 1948.[26]

Again, for such a dramatic and impactful revolution, it lasted no more than three days and was conducted by no more than a hundred junior-ranking officers of the army. The swiftness and the ease with which the Free Officers succeeded were the results of various pieces of the revolution falling into place: the rapid growing, reorganization, and restructuring of the Free Officers by Gamal Abdel Nasser in the late 1940s and early 1950s; the increasing woes of the Egyptian people and burgeoning discontent for the continuing occupation and deteriorating political and economic order; and the lack of a strong state-controlled military that could be effectively mobilized against an oncoming force from within.[27]

Sadat himself was overjoyed at the swiftness and nonviolence of the revolution. He had performed notable tasks during it, and his voice and name were known to most of Egypt as the one who had announced the success of the revolution. As he recalled in his memoir, "Then came the 1952 revolution in which I took part. My participation was not in itself a matter of importance to me. Of more import than anything else was the fact that the revolution had been carried out. The dream that had taken hold of my life ever since I was a child of barely twelve years had come true."[28]

Chapter 2: President Gamal Abdel Nasser

Much has been written about Anwar Sadat's relationship with Gamal Abdel Nasser. In the eighteen years that the two friends worked together to topple and rebuild the Egyptian state, not once did the two have a falling out, unlike all of the other notable officials and supporters who

---

[26] Elie Podeh and Onn Winckler, "Introduction: Nasserism as a Form of Populism," in *Rethinking Nasserism: Revolution and Historical Memory in Modern* Egypt, ed. Elie Podeh and Onn Winckler (Gainesville, FL: University Press of Florida, 2004), 2-3.
[27] Joel Gordon, *Nasser's Blessed Movement: Egypt's Free Officers and the July Revolution* (New York: Oxford University Press, 1992), 39.
[28] El-Sadat, *Those I Have Known,* 80.

had worked under Nasser. A journalist in London approached Anwar Sadat with this very question – how were you able to spend such a long period with Nasser, without quarreling, or disagreeing, or becoming estranged from the vociferous and often excessively dynamic Nasser? Sadat, in his autobiography *Those I Have Known*, wrote that the journalist finally concluded that Sadat had been "either of absolutely no consequence or so cunning" that he managed to avoid falling out with Nasser. Sadat disagreed with this assessment, and proceeded to explain the true nature of his relationship with the first president of the Egyptian Republic: "If the naïve perplexity of those people is proof of anything, it is simply proof of their ignorance of my nature. For I was neither inconsequential during Nasser's lifetime nor shy or cunning at any point in mine. The matter is quite simple. Nasser and I became friends at the age of nineteen. Then came the revolution. He became president of the Republic. I was glad, for the friend I trusted had become president and that made me happy. I felt exactly the same way when Nasser became a hallowed leader of the Arab nation. At times we would differ, and then we would become estranged, sometimes for two months or even more. This would be due either to our differences of opinion or to the machinations of those with influence on him, for Nasser had a natural tendency to lend an ear to gossip."[29]

The relationship between Sadat and Nasser was therefore not as sturdy as those around them thought, nor was Sadat himself completely subordinate to Nasser. The two often had disagreements, and as Sadat recalled, they at times became estranged, sometimes months at a time. Some believed the two to be the best of friends – mutually loyal, committed, and respectful. Yet, this was also not always the case; Sadat described the relationship was "certainly not one of friendship," though they did have "mutual respect and trust."[30]

It could be said that Sadat became the trusted companion of Nasser, the vice president of Egypt, then eventually the successor to Nasser as president of Egypt not necessarily solely because of his relationship with Nasser, but because of his quiet demeanor and skilled abilities to detect, observe, and maneuver among the various strong personalities, egos, and mindsets that made up the nascent Egyptian government. His daughter Camelia Anwar Sadat wrote in a tribute to him that her father "envisioned and planned, but he did not overwhelm people with his insights and strength. He preferred to keep his views to himself. He never showed his power. This was a response to his environment growing up, an environment in which showing power often invited confrontation."[31]

Yet as respectful and trusting Sadat's relationship with Nasser was, the same could not be said for his relationship with the other influential figures in the post-revolution government. In the months that followed the success of the 1952 Egyptian Revolution, Sadat gradually began to see, to his dismay, that many of his colleagues in the Constituent Committee were nothing but self-

---

[29] El-Sadat, *Those I Have Known*, 75.
[30] Ibid., 70.
[31] Sadat and El-Sayed, "Anwar Sadat and His Vision," 5.

centered opportunists, each seeking to gain more power at the expense of others. Perhaps it was no surprise that he suddenly found himself among bigots and sycophants; many of these figures on the Committee had been previously low- or mid-ranking army officers – as most of the members of the Free Officers Movement were – and they had each known poverty and injustice; yet, they were suddenly catapulted to positions of great power and influence in the newly formed government. Young, ambitious, and above all, self-interested, these Committee members appeared to care more about their own personal advancement than for the future of the nation.

At first, Sadat was too focused on the victory of the revolution, but he gradually came to realize that he was the object of considerable animosity, envy, or likely a mixture of both among his colleagues. Much of it had to do with the fact that it had been Anwar Sadat, and not Nasser or any of the other leaders of the Free Officers, who had announced the revolution to the country and delivered the ultimatum to King Farouk, forcing his departure. Sadat was therefore the only Committee member who was known to the public and the media, and thus there were some who were discontent with his highly visible role. It was with this realization that Sadat came to refuse any involvement in the power struggles and quarrels for titles that the others engaged in.

Sadat's disengagement from the internal politics of rule, however, allowed the others to try to turn Nasser against him. Nasser was inherently a deeply suspicious man, often lending an ear to rumors and gossip, not knowing such stories might have been contrived by the very person who was feeding him the information; as Sadat recalled, Nasser was "the eternal doubter, cautious, full of bitterness, high-strung."[32] Whenever Nasser became cold toward him or lost contact with him for several weeks or months, Sadat would simply draw on his experience of solitary confinement at the Cairo prison and remember that his own integrity and belief in the revolution were the only things that mattered.

As Sadat recalled in his autobiography, he was shuffled around in various positions during the presidency of Nasser, eventually ending up as vice president. Yet, it appeared he did not mind being appointed to different positions, nor was he particularly concerned about advancement. He wrote, "It is that which made me live with Nasser for eighteen years without strife. For I wanted nothing. I had no demands of any kind, no matter what my position, whether as a member of the Revolutionary Council, or secretary of the Islamic Conference, or editor-in-chief of the newspaper *al-Goumhouria,* or Deputy Speaker of the National Assembly, or even Speaker of the National assembly. My love for Nasser never changed; my feelings toward him never altered. I was by his side whether in victory or defeat. Maybe that is what made Nasser look around him after eighteen years and wake up to the fact that there was one person with whom he had never once fallen out."[33]

On September 7, 1952, Prime Minister Ali Maher Pasha, who had been appointed by the

---

[32] El-Sadat, *Those I Have Known,* 79.
[33] Ibid., 80.

Revolutionary Council to form a new government, resigned over differences with the council.[34] In Maher's stead, Major General Muhammad Naguib was appointed. Soon after, an anti-government plot – formed by some of the old politicians who had been stripped of much of their pre-revolution powers, in conjunction with several ambitious army officers – was discovered; the response that the Revolutionary Council took was severe. All those suspected of involvement in the plot were swiftly arrested and the officers court martialed, and the council assumed all legislative and executive power for the next three years.[35] On January 16, 1953, the council also dissolved and banned all political parties in the country, and the Muslim Brotherhood – an Islamist group with strong roots in Egypt, with which Anwar Sadat himself previously was involved prior to the revolution – was also outlawed and forced underground. In 1953, the monarchy was officially abolished, Egypt became a republic, and Muhammad Naguib was announced as the republic's first president and prime minister. Nasser was declared deputy premier and interior minister, though in truth, as the one with all the power and influence, he was already by this point the true leader of the republic of Egypt.[36]

Ali Maher Pasha

By the end of the year, the nascent revolutionary regime could already point to some proud accomplishments; the 1952 Agrarian Reform Law had led to a major land redistribution program and limited land ownership to around 200 acres, distributing previously unobtainable plots of

---

[34] Elbendary, "The Long Revolution."
[35] Carroll, *Anwar Sadat*, 36.
[36] Elbendary, "The Long Revolution."

land to landless farmers. The property of the royal family had been confiscated, and the money was used to build hospitals and schools in rural areas and fund infrastructure projects.[37] Politicians and officials of the old regime were swiftly tried and sentenced by a revolutionary tribunal, of which Anwar Sadat was a part of.[38] It appeared the new republic was well on its way to development and growth.

Possibly the biggest accomplishment for Nasser and his regime, and for Sadat as well, was the signing of the Anglo-Egyptian Evacuation Agreement on October 19, 1954. Even after the revolution and the ouster of the king, British troops and advisors had remained in the country. By 1954, the revolutionary leaders could no longer stall one of the biggest objectives they had had in bringing about the revolution; Nasser embarked on negotiations for the withdrawal of all British troops. The British submitted their terms – they wished to maintain their hold on the Suez Canal base for another 24 months, then retain some of their stores and about 1,200 civilian experts in Egypt for the next seven years. Nasser was eager to hear the views of his advisors; a lengthy meeting was held, and council members began arguing over the most minute of details, much to Sadat's annoyance. It is said that the frustrated Sadat finally burst out saying, "What is there to be discussed? The British want to retain some 1,200 non-military experts who would thus be guarded by us, the Egyptians, will such experts frighten us?...Only a stupid politician could reject such a solution to a problem that is over seventy-five years old."[39]

The council agreed, and the draft was accepted. The last British soldier left Egyptian soil on June 19, 1956, and the revolutionary government was finally able to herald the end of the British occupation of Egypt.[40]

At the same time, the 1950s were times of growing animosity between the U.S. and the Soviet Union, marking the beginnings of the Cold War. As Nasser and Sadat maneuvered through the dangerous game of nation-building in a world dominated by the superpower rivalry, Nasser's government became the model of non-alignment. Egypt came to represent the voices of the undeveloped, underdeveloped, and post-colonial nations of the world, which wished to stay free of the developing U.S.-Soviet rift.

The British had left Egypt relatively peacefully, but it was by no means satisfied with its loss of influence in the key country. In order to retain its control over the region, British Prime Minister Anthony Eden began discussions for the creation of what became known as the 1955 Baghdad Pact, designed to create an alliance with pro-Western states in the Middle East. Iraq, Turkey, Iran, and Pakistan were quick to come on board, eager to strengthen their defenses during a time when the Soviet Union's infiltration into the Middle East was a very real threat. Nasser was infuriated that Britain would even ask for Egypt's entry into the pact, as was Sadat;

---

[37] Carroll, *Anwar Sadat*, 38.
[38] Elbendary, "The Long Revolution."
[39] Carroll, *Anwar Sadat*, 41.
[40] Alagna, *Anwar Sadat*, 44.

Nasser voiced his strong opposition to the Baghdad Pact through fiery speeches broadcasted by the Voice of Arabs radio in Cairo, and his strong opposition and the popular support Nasser enjoyed in other neighboring Arab countries led to Syria and Jordan declining signing into the pact.[41]

Sadat himself played a key role; one of his positions at the time was secretary-general of the Islamic Congress – a pan-Arab organization established to further relations among Arab states. As its head, Sadat flew from country to country, meeting with heads of states and ministers of each and convincing them that they should stay clear of the pact. Additionally, by this time, Sadat was also editor-in-chief of a national newspaper, *al-Goumhouria*, and as such, he used his role in the media aptly by continuously publishing articles highly critical of the pact, some of which he wrote himself.[42]

Egypt's strong opposition against the pact irked not only Britain, but also its ally, the United States. When Egypt proposed a weapons deal with the U.S., hoping for a strictly financial deal, it discovered that the U.S. was only interested in political alliances, offering their weapons for free in exchange for Egyptian loyalty and an American presence in Egypt. Nasser was greatly angered; he had no intention of placing Egypt under the influence and control of a Western power so soon after it had finally liberated itself from Britain. Though an arms deal with the Soviet Union also initially fell through, in 1955, Soviet Premier Nikita Khrushchev finally signed a deal, cementing military ties between Cairo and Moscow.[43]

---

[41] Gerald Butt, "Lesson From History: 1955 Baghdad Pact," *BBC News*, February 26, 2003, http://news.bbc.co.uk/2/hi/middle_east/2801487.stm.
[42] Carroll, *Anwar Sadat*, 15.
[43] Ibid., 39.

Khrushchev

In early 1956, Nasser announced a new constitution, setting up a presidential system of government. Several months later, in June 1956, Nasser was elected president of Egypt in a national plebiscite. Consequently, the three-year rule of the Revolutionary Council ended, and the council was dissolved. Though Sadat was pleased with Nasser's victory, he was disturbed by the level of petty bickering and rivalries that many of the power-hungry government officials were engaged in. Though he congratulated Nasser sincerely, he told him that he did not want a post in the new government.[44]

Egypt's most important trial as a newly established republic, and as beacon of the post-colonial

---
[44] Ibid., 46.

non-alignment countries, came in 1956. The much-anticipated Aswan High Dam project had been underway, and many Western countries and international organizations, such as the U.S., France, Britain, and the World Bank, had agreed to help finance it, promising funds of approximately $70 million.[45] However, the 1955 arms deal with the Soviet Union had been a slap to the face for the U.S.; though Egypt had been strictly looking to build up its defenses, and not necessarily attempting to establish political and military ties with the enemy of the Americans, the U.S. viewed the deal as Cairo choosing a side in the looming Cold War. The U.S. swiftly called on its allies to back out of the dam project, effectively withholding the money needed to complete it.[46] Within days, the Soviet Union saw its chance and swiftly offered to finance the High Dam project, further earning the animosity of the Western states, but boosting Nasser's confidence and Egypt's morale.

On July 26, 1956, in one of the most historic speeches that stunned the nation and the world, Gamal Abdel Nasser announced the nationalization of the Suez Canal. The move was unprecedented and thought impossible, as the canal was built and owned by a British and French consortium; yet, Nasser simply declared it to be the property of Egypt, and announced that its revenues would now be taken by Egypt to fund the Aswan High Dam project.

Sadat was aghast, as was the rest of the world. As much pride as he felt in the fact that his country and its leader had stood up to its long-time former colonizer, he was greatly disturbed by the consequences such a move would bring. It is highly likely that if he had known about Nasser's intention – which according to him, he did not – he would have heavily opposed the brash and certainly reckless move. To Sadat, defying the British meant war, which was not too far off a conclusion. Though popular opinion of Nasser skyrocketed, Sadat feared for the worst, as the Egyptian military was hardly prepared for an all-out war with the Western alliance.

Just as Sadat feared, in October of 1956, Britain, France, and Israel struck Egypt simultaneously – Israel from the ground, and the British and French from the air – seizing key bases in the Sinai, and in one swift sweep, bombarding all the aircraft that Egypt had bought from the Soviets.[47] Egypt hastily asked for aid from the Soviet Union, which pointedly refused. It was this unpredictability of the Soviet Union during the Suez crisis that made Sadat grow distrustful of Moscow, later impacting his foreign policy during his own presidency.

Aid finally came not from the Soviet Union, nor from neighboring Arab countries, but from the most unexpected country: the United States. Angered by the fact that the leader of the democratic bloc and Western alliance had not been forewarned about this tripartite aggression, U.S. President Dwight D. Eisenhower demanded that the three countries immediately halt their advance and withdraw their troops. Britain, France, and Israel – just as surprised about the

---

[45] Elbendary, "The Long Revolution."
[46] Alagna, *Anwar Sadat*, 16.
[47] Carroll, *Anwar Sadat*, 47.

forcefulness of the U.S. as Egypt was – had no choice but to comply. Egypt won full control of the Suez Canal, though without the intervention of the U.S., it would have certainly been defeated.

Sadat was also astonished by Eisenhower's actions, and at the same time, he saw a perfect opportunity for Egypt to establish stronger ties with the U.S. Though he advised Nasser to pursue such a course, no such ties were made, and Egyptian-U.S. relations reverted back to the pre-crisis status quo. This may be one of the key differences between Gamal Abdel Nasser and Anwar Sadat, as people, as leaders, and as Egyptian presidents; Nasser often let not only his own hubris, but also the pride of others to get in the way of strategic thinking. In an era when Nasser was being touted as the pan-Arab leader, the epitome of what every Arab country's president should be like, he was somewhat enthralled by his own image and determined to maintain it. The advisors he surrounded himself with were much the same – concerned more about self-interests and reputation. This is in contrast to Sadat, who disliked bickering over details but found his strength in always keeping in mind the big picture, and constantly thinking of the future of Egypt instead of just the present. The Soviet Union had proved itself to be an unreliable ally, if one could even call it that; closer relations with the U.S. would have benefited Egypt greatly in the long-run. Yet, Nasser refused to explore those options, and Sadat became convinced that "Nasser's judgment was being warped by pro-Soviet advisors who flattered and cajoled a man who was increasingly taken with his own myth as world leader."[48]

The posts that Nasser had appointed Sadat to had been prominent and influential, deserving of a loyal supporter and friend, but not ones that provided any real power bases. The National Assembly, the Islamic Congress, and the editorship of a newspaper were not posts that could ever be a launching pad for Sadat to challenge the presidency. It was for this reason that it was perhaps Sadat who was most surprised when Nasser appointed him vice president in 1964.

Sadat revealed very little about the circumstances that led to Nasser's decision. With the possible exception of Sadat himself, Nasser never revealed to anyone the clear reasons behind Sadat's appointment, though perhaps the individual who got the most complete account may be journalist Mohamed Hassanein Heikal, editor-in-chief of the renowned Cairo newspaper *Al-Ahram* and a commentator respected not only in Egypt and the Middle East, but across the world. A personal friend of Nasser's and minister in his administration, but widely known for his rocky relationship with Sadat, Heikal has written about the day he was told by Nasser that he had appointed Sadat as vice president. According to Heikal, Nasser had chosen Sadat because he saw in him "the least aggressive of his Cabinet and the least likely to betray in order to obtain power for himself."[49] This is corroborated by Sadat's own analysis of Nasser's personality – always suspicious, doubtful, and quick to lend an ear to gossips and rumors.

---

[48] Ibid., 48.
[49] Joseph Finklestone, *Anwar Sadat: Visionary Who Dared*, 49.

However, the details of the conversation that Heikal had with Nasser regarding Sadat's appointment paint a very unappealing picture of Sadat and likely biased version of events, though there are few, if any, ways to confirm this. According to Heikal, he had been chatting with Nasser as he accompanied him on his journey to the Arab Summit in Rabat, Morocco. As they were taking their seats in the plane, Nasser said with a light laugh, "Do you know what I did today? Sadat was coming to see me off at the airport, so I told him to make certain that he brought a Koran along with him – I think he took the hint. I have sworn him in as Vice-President while I am out of Egypt."[50]

When a baffled Heikal asked Nasser why he had chosen Sadat, Nasser reportedly handed him a stack of telegrams from an advance party sent to Rabat to secure the sites Nasser was staying in. Among the reports was one that stated that the Moroccan Interior Minister, General Mohammed Okfir, was collaborating with the CIA to execute a plan to assassinate Nasser during his stay in Rabat. Nasser wanted to ensure that if anything were to happen to him on this trip, there would be someone who would at least be able to keep warm the seat of the president without bringing down the government; Sadat's role as president, if it ever did come to this, would be ceremonial. Furthermore, according to Heikal, Nasser then added that, "Besides, all the others have been Vice-President at one time or another; it's Anwar's turn."[51]

Heikal's account implies that Nasser had a negative image of Sadat as weak, or simply as a placeholder, but this is likely a distorted view, especially given Heikal's difficult relationship with Sadat. Sadat himself had stayed largely quiet about the reasons Nasser gave for appointing him – if he *did* give any reasons, that is. It may very well be that only Nasser himself knew the true reasons behind his decision, which is very fitting for a leader with a personality revolving around paranoia and constant suspicion. Nonetheless, regardless of the speculation surrounding the *why*, the *what* was very clear. Anwar Sadat became Vice President of the Republic of Egypt on February 17, 1964. He would serve two terms before succeeding Nasser as president.

The final momentous event of Nasser's presidency was the 1967 Six Day War, fought between Israel and a coalition of Arab states, including Egypt. The great debacle that this war would bring about for Egypt impacted Nasser severely, as well as Sadat. Field Marshal Abdel Hakim Amer, a good friend of Nasser's who had rose within the ranks of the military largely due to his friendship with the president, was the commander in chief of the armed forces. Sadat had never been too fond of Amer; the man was greedy, power-hungry, and surrounded by followers who fed his ego more than his mind. For example, it had been discovered in 1965 that Amer and his subordinates had been abusing their power and using unlawful and brutal methods against members of the Muslim Brotherhood, and even against those who had nothing to do with the Brotherhood, but were merely "suspected" of involvement in the banned Islamist organization. Sadat had urged Nasser to remove Amer from his post, but Nasser was unable to act against his

---

[50] Ibid., 63.
[51] Ibid., 64.

good friend.[52] This was who the armed forces were being led by as war with Israel began to loom in the late 1960s.

Nasser was under strong pressure from other Arab states to join in the increasing hostilities against Israel, which had in late 1966, began engaging Jordanian troops in sporadic conflicts. Arab states urged Nasser to close the Strait of Tiran – Israel's only outlet to international waters. Boosted by rising popular expectations of Arab, and particularly Egyptian, military might, on May 18, 1967, Nasser demanded the withdrawal of the United Nations Emergency Force (UNEF) stationed in Egypt's side of its border with Israel in the Sinai. The Straits of Tiran was closed, and Egypt signed a defense pact with Jordan and Syria.[53]

Israeli attacks on Egyptian forces began in earnest on June 5. The undefended Egyptian air force was wiped out on the ground after a strategically targeted air raid by Israeli forces. Nasser was baffled about why his air force had been completely undefended; Amer blamed the U.S., alleging that American planes had joined and swept the ground in the air raid, but Nasser and all others knew where the true fault lay. Amer then abruptly ordered a full withdrawal of Egyptian troops – an order Sadat branded "as being, in effect, an order to commit suicide."[54] A bewildered Nasser demanded to know why Amer did not attempt to establish a defense line in the Sinai; Amer replied that the line – which was to be ready at all times – had not been ready.[55] In the days that followed, Israeli troops were easily able to march across the Sinai, meeting little resistance from the Egyptians who were deprived of all air cover. By June 9, Sadat knew it was all over – most of the towns and cities of the Sinai had been seized by Israeli forces, and on June 10, Israel captured the Golan Heights. A ceasefire was signed on June 11, and as the humiliation of the defeat sunk in, Nasser offered to abdicate, but upon hearing Sadat and the people call for his continued leadership, he decided to stay on. Field Marshal Amer was promptly placed under house arrest for his ineptitude as commander-in-chief, and he later committed suicide.[56]

---

[52] Carroll, *Anwar Sadat*, 51.
[53] Elbendary, "The Long Revolution."
[54] Sullivan, *Sadat: The Man Who Changed Mid-East History*, 53.
[55] Carroll, *Anwar Sadat*, 52.
[56] Ibid., 55.

Amer

Sadat was intent on discovering the truth of why his nation and leader had failed, as he could not bring himself to believe that it was because of cowardice or lack of skills on the part of the Egyptian soldiers. After the war, he launched a full investigation that he himself largely led, interviewing brigade members and officers. He eventually discovered that it was not cowardice, lack of training, or general ineptitude of the soldiers that had led to the defeat; there had been mix ups and confusion on the ground, with conflicting orders issued to the brigades. Indecision among the military leadership had apparently been rampant. Sadat concluded that it was not the incompetence of the soldiers, or the lack of training or weaponry; the problem lay in the leadership.[57] He subsequently began work on the restructuring and strengthening of the Egyptian military.

Raw hatred for Israel is a common feature among Arab leaders, and one that Nasser himself could not escape. The Suez crisis had emboldened him; though it had been the U.S. who had orchestrated the withdrawal of foreign forces from the Canal Zone, Nasser and much of Egypt genuinely believed that it was Egypt that had won that crisis. Yet, the lack of organization and the sheer number of missteps that the Egyptian army, the leadership, and Nasser himself took during those ill-fated six days were an indication that Egypt and its allies were not even close to being fully prepared for a full-fledged war.

As the purportedly most powerful nation in the Arab world, defeat in a war that had only lasted six days was a devastation to the reputation and image of Egypt. But more than this, the

---

[57] Sullivan, *Sadat: The Man Who Changed Mid-East History*, 56.

humiliation that Nasser felt was severe; his pride had been dealt a crippling blow, from which he would never fully recover. He changed physically as well: "Nasser's appearance changed drastically. His eyes turned dull. His smile no longer dazzled. His face and hands took on a sickly pallor. Death seemed to be stalking him."[58]

And perhaps death had truly been stalking him. Three years later, on September 28, 1970, Gamal Abdel Nasser died at his residence in Cairo of a heart attack. His funeral was momentous and emotional; mourners filled the streets of Cairo and cities across Egypt, weeping over the departure of their revolutionary leader. Anwar Sadat, as the vice president, automatically became acting president.

Chapter 3: Sadat's Presidency

Sadat and the Shah of Iran in 1975

Sadat wrote in his autobiography, "We [Nasser and I] both shared the same fears about what might happen in Egypt after Nasser's departure. Nasser concurred with me that great burdens were waiting his successor, and I laughed and told him: 'Allah will have to help the poor fellow'...It certainly never crossed out minds that Nasser would die in that very same month, of that I would be taking over in a new process of transferring power. But that was the will of Allah."[59]

---

[58] Ibid., 54.
[59] El-Sadat, *Those I Have Known*, 82.

Indeed, the presidency was thrown suddenly and unexpectedly at Sadat, and he initially had much trouble deciding what to do with it. To his critics, he was perceived as weak and unimpressive, always standing in the shadow of Nasser, his calls for retaliation against Israel and promises for the revitalization of Egypt deemed hollow and contrived. Likewise, he was seen as a transitional leader abroad, as a caretaker – someone simply keeping the seat warm as Egypt organized a new round of elections. Elliot Richardson, whom President Richard Nixon had sent to Cairo to attend Nasser's funeral, reported to Washington that Sadat would not be president for any more than four to six weeks before someone more fitting was elected or selected.[60]

Of course, Sadat would prove them all wrong. He had inherited possibly the worst state a country could ever be in – a populace still dragging the humiliation of a quick and devastating defeat, a crippled economy, chaotic foreign relations, and a government filled with factions, intrigue, squabbles, and conflicts. His critics and political enemies expected him to reel before the overwhelming burdens; instead, the poor village lad turned leading revolutionary, who had endured long years of solitary confinement and survived it all through sheer determination and passion, would show that he and only he could pick up Egypt from where it fell.

The constitution of Egypt allowed up to sixty days for a new president to be selected, but this was not needed; nine days after Nasser's death, the National Assembly formally elected Sadat as the new president of Egypt. The following week, Sadat won 90.4% of the vote in a national referendum. Anwar Sadat was sworn into the office of president for a six-year term.[61]

It was somewhat of a truth that Sadat was not truly the leader of Egypt when he took office. The real power in Egypt was staunchly in the hands of three other government officials who had been senior advisors to Nasser, and who considered themselves to be the rightful heirs. The first was Sami Sharaf, the presidential affairs minister; the second was Sharawi Gomah, the powerful Interior Minister, and the third was Ali Sabri, who headed Egypt's air defense system.[62] These men were proud, well-established, experienced, and had been playing the game for a long time; they expected Sadat to be a pushover, or at the very least, they expected to be able to retain their status and powers that they had enjoyed during Nasser administration.

Yet Sadat was no Nasser, as they soon found out. Whereas Nasser valued intuition and often ruled on his own personal whim or that of others, Sadat was a firm believer in the rule of law and establishing a proper, accountable system of governance. One instance of his personality occurred on his first day in office, when he was brought a pile of transcripts of tapped personal telephone conversations. Initially perplexed, he went through them, only to discover that they had nothing to do with state affairs or security, but was just another product of Nasser's obsessive concern for his own personal security. Sadat ordered an immediate halt to wiretapping,

---

[60] Carroll, *Anwar Sadat*, 60.
[61] Sullivan, *Sadat: The Man Who Changed Mid-East History*, 82-83.
[62] Ibid., 64-65.

except in cases of national security, and then only through a court order.[63]

Thus, Sadat was determined to bring back – or rather, establish from scratch – order and regulation within the government. He therefore launched what he called the Corrective Revolution on May 15, 1971, through which he embarked on purging the government and security forces of all Nasserites, especially those who were pro-Soviet. He first removed Ali Sabri, the chief of the air defense system who was known to have close ties to the Soviet Union, from his position. Next, Sharawi Gomah was dismissed, triggering a mass resignation of top-level government officials who were loyal to Sabri and Gomah. Unexpected to those who resigned, who had expected Sadat to falter in the face of these mass resignations, Sadat crisply accepted the resignations, made the news public, and placed the entire group under house arrest. That very night, Sadat formed a new government, filling the now empty positions with those he deemed were loyal to Egypt first rather than to the Soviet Union or their own self-interests.[64]

The move against the corrupt and the powerful won him cheers from the populace. Sadat's popularity soared even higher when he cut back the powers of the much-hated secret police and set about dismantling the police state created by Nasser and his pro-Soviet advisors.[65] The Corrective Revolution was indeed a great success in terms of the immense approval he received from his people, an also in terms of setting himself apart from the harsh and closed-off rule of Nasser. It demonstrated Sadat's intuitive grasp of what his people truly wanted, and his willingness to give them exactly that; political prisons were permanently shut down, tapes and transcripts of private telephone conversations held by the Interior Ministry were destroyed, and the arbitrary arrests that had become so rampant during Nasser 's rule were halted.

Sadat continued to have difficult relations with the Soviet Union. Ever since the Suez crisis and the Soviet Union's clear refusal to come to Egypt's aid, Sadat had been greatly suspicious of the superpower and its intentions. Since Sadat took the presidency, various negotiations were held with the Soviets, and several treaties were signed, but these were mostly to mollify the Soviet Union and keep its leaders from discerning Sadat's true stance toward his fickle ally. Relations between the two countries continued to deteriorate. Weapons deals were made, but the weapons never arrived. Soviet politburo members promised him arms, but they never came. Sadat traveled to Moscow numerous times to inquire about these promised weapons, but he was always brushed off and returned home empty-handed.

In July 1972, Sadat surprised his nation, the region, and the world when he abruptly ordered all 15,000 Soviet advisors and military experts stationed in Egypt to leave the country within a week. Sadat also demanded all Soviet equipment to be sold to Egypt, or to also be taken out of Egypt within a week. An angry Moscow responded by recalling all of its citizens and equipment,

---

[63] Carroll, *Anwar Sadat*, 61.
[64] Ibid., 63.
[65] Eric Pace, "Anwar El-Sadat, the Daring Arab Pioneer of Peace with Israel," *The New York Times,* October 7, 1981, http://www.nytimes.com/learning/general/onthisday/bday/1225.html.

flying them back to the Soviet Union in haste.[66] The move was so unexpected that it surprised even the United States, as Sadat had asked for nothing from the U.S. in exchange for expelling the Soviet advisors.

As impulsive as Sadat's exasperated decision to teach the Soviets a lesson may have been, it was also deemed necessary from a long-terms perspective. It was becoming clear to Sadat that the Soviet Union was using arms supplies and deals as a means of controlling Egyptian foreign policy, and Moscow's arrogant and condescending attitude toward Cairo did nothing to ameliorate the situation, instead exacerbating it to such a degree that Sadat was forced to take action. The move was immensely popular with his people; yet again, he was correcting past wrongs and truly taking into account the will of the Egyptian people.

Also known as the October War or the Ramadan War, the 1973 Yom Kippur War was the culmination of the efforts made by Sadat and Syrian president Hafez Assad to regain the territories lost to Israel in 1967 – the Golan Heights, the Sinai Peninsula, Gaza Strip, and the West Bank. The magnitude of the Israeli victory during the 1967 Six Day War and the sheer humiliation that the Arab states had experienced suggested that the Arabs would need many years, possibly even decades, before it could embark on another major armed conflict to regain the territories lost. And indeed, as history witnessed, neither Egypt nor Syria was ready for war.

---

[66] Carroll, *Anwar Sadat*, 65

Hafez Assad

Sadat had given no signs of his intention to engage in another war with Israel. On February 4, 1971, Sadat launched what he called a peace imitative in a speech to the National Assembly, designed to obtain Israel's full withdrawal from the Suez Canal zone, the reopening of the waterway, and a lasting ceasefire. Throughout 1971, Sadat, his Israeli counterparts, and U.S. officials led by U.S. Secretary of State Henry Kissinger worked tirelessly to come to an agreement for the terms of such an initiative, but both the Egyptian and the Israeli leaders experienced roadblocks with each other and with members of their own government. Though even declaring his readiness to make peace with Israel was a daring and courageous departure from historically anti-Israeli Arab political rhetoric, negotiations stalled. By May 1971, after only three months of trying for a peaceful solution, Sadat concluded that war was his only option.[67]

---

[67] Benny Morris, *Righteous Victims: A History of the Zionist-Arab Conflict, 1881-1998* (New York: Vintage Books, 1999), 388-390.

Kissinger

Whether patient diplomacy could have in time achieved a peace agreement remains a matter of speculation; most analysts believe that the steadily plummeting morale of his people and decreasing popularity of Sadat's engagement with the Israelis would have made a continuation of peace efforts unlikely. Jehan, Sadat's wife, later told an Israeli newspaper in 1987 that peace could never have been achieved without the two countries first passing through the trials of war.[68] In addition to this was the problem of morale. As historian Abraham Rabinovich wrote, "The three years since Sadat had taken office – a period of no war, no peace – were the most

---

[68] Abraham Rabinovich, *The Yom Kippur War: The Epic Encounter that Transformed the Middle East* (New York: Schocken Books, 2004), 13.

demoralized in modern Egyptian history…A deep sense of humiliation and helplessness was reflected in literature and song and in the sardonic jokes about the army and the national leadership, particularly Sadat. A desiccated economy added to the nation's despondency."[69]

By June 1971, Sadat was steadily veering away from the path of peace; he declared that he was willing to "sacrifice a million Egyptian soldiers" to recover the lands lost to Israel.[70] At first, Sadat had decided on a specific date – November 15, 1972 – to launch an offensive against Israel in the occupied Sinai Peninsula. Yet, administrative and logistical mishaps led to the postponement of this date. Full mobilization was ordered in Egypt, Syria, and Israel.

Sadat developed a war strategy that differed from that employed by his predecessor during the Six Day War. Nasser had had no faith in the U.S. from the outset; he had worked with the Soviets, relying on them and strengthening the two countries' ties. On the other hand, Sadat deeply mistrusted the Soviets – a mistrust that was exacerbated by failed arms deals and unfulfilled promises of weapons and supplies until culminating in the expulsion of thousands of Soviet military advisors from Egypt.

In fact, by casting away the Soviets, Sadat had created an opening for the possible establishment of ties with the U.S. However, the world, including both the Soviets and the Americans, had misinterpreted Sadat's intentions, believing that by throwing out the Soviets, Sadat was giving up all thoughts of another war with Israel. The decision had been received with sheer dismay in Moscow, delight in Israel, and confusion in the U.S.; all three eventually concluded that Egypt would not be going to war in the foreseeable future, and thus, the U.S. disregarded the development.

No one – not even most Egyptians – realized that Sadat's move to expel the Soviets was intended to invite the Americans in, in the hopes that they would become more involved as the mediator in the conflict and pressure Israel. If that failed – which indeed, it did – Sadat was set on going to war, in which case a massive Soviet presence in Egypt would be an impediment more than an advantage, given Moscow's known opposition to any conflict between Egypt and Israel. Sadat waited, but Washington failed to fill the vacuum left by the Soviets. He had no choice but to reach out to the Soviets again, and Soviet military assistance eventually resumed in early 1973.[71]

On October 1, 1973, five days before the start of the war, Sadat outlined his strategies in a directive issued to his war minister and commander-in-chief, General Ahmad Ismail Ali: "To challenge the Israeli Security Theory by carrying out a military action according to the capabilities of the armed forces aimed at inflicting the heaviest losses on the enemy and convincing him that continued occupation of our land exacts a price too high for him to pay, and

---

[69] Ibid.
[70] Morris, *Righteous Victims: A History of the Zionist-Arab Conflict, 1881-1998*, 390.
[71] Carroll, *Anwar Sadat*, 66

that consequently his theory of security—based as it is on psychological, political, and military intimidation—is not an impregnable shield of steel which could protect him today or in the future. A successful challenge of the Israeli Security Theory will have definite short-term and long-term consequences. In the short term, a challenge to the Israeli Security Theory could have a certain result, which would make it possible for an honorable solution for the Middle East crisis to be reached. In the long-term, a challenge to the Israeli Security Theory can produce changes which will, following on the heels of one another, lead to a basic change in the enemy's thinking, morale, and aggressive tendencies."[72]

The "Israeli Security Theory" that Sadat repeatedly mentioned was a widely used term in Egypt that described what most Egyptians considered to be the main obstacle to peace in the Middle East: Israel's unchallenged and so far proven belief that it could deter any and all Arab attempts to regain lost territories and defeat Israel militarily. In the eyes of Sadat and much of Egypt, this belief had hardened into a truth in Israeli minds, as the sheer strength and invincibility of the Israel Defense Forces (IDF) were proven during the 1967 war. As much as Sadat hoped for a peaceful resolution to the conflict, he believed that it was this Israeli mindset that was preventing peace talks, and to soften Israel's intransigence toward the negotiations, the Israeli Security Theory must be disproven through a successful Egyptian military operation and Arab victory in war.

To do this, Sadat ordered his war minister to focus not on seizing strategic bases or cutting off supply lines, but on exacting a psychological effect on the people of Israel by causing as many casualties as possible. In fact, when General Ali asked for a clarification, Sadat clearly stated that a chief objective of the war was "to inflict on the enemy the greatest possible losses in men, weapons, and equipment."[73] In an interview with *Newsweek* published on April 9, 1973, just six months before the war, Sadat disclosed his belief that war was inevitable, even if negotiations were to continue: "The time has come for a shock. Diplomacy will continue before, during, and after the battle. All west Europeans are telling us that everybody has fallen asleep over the Middle East crisis. But they will soon wake up to the fact that America has left us no other way out. The resumption of the hostilities is the only way out. Everything is now being mobilized in concert for the resumption of the battle which is inevitable."[74]

Additionally, in his autobiography, *In Search of Identity*, Sadat wrote, "Israeli military successes had created a false picture. Contrary to popular conception, they were not invincible and we were not inept. I had to win back honor and prestige for my people – not only in Egypt but throughout the Arab world. It would be necessary to inflict losses on Israel. The myth that they were unbeatable had grown, but I knew the reality: Israel is a small country, little able to

---

[72] George W. Gawrych, *The 1973 Arab Israeli War: The Albatross of Decisive Victory* (Combat Studies Institute, U.S. Army Command and General Staff College, 1996), 12.
[73] Ibid., 13.
[74] Boaz Vanetik and Zaki Shalom, "The White House Middle East Policy in 1973 as a Catalyst for the Outbreak of the Yom Kippur War," *Israeli Studies* 16, no. 1 (2011): 67.

suffer a significant loss of soldiers, property, and equipment. I needed to affect the psyche of the Israelis to make them understand that territory alone provides no real security."[75]

It was in this environment that on October 6, 1973 – the day of Yom Kippur, the holiest day in the Jewish calendar – Egypt and Syria launched a coordinated surprise attack against Israel. A commonly held misconception is that Israel provoked the Arab states into war, but as has been discussed, Sadat had been hinting at a military engagement months before Yom Kippur, and by September, final training exercises had been completed by Egyptian troops and navy units had already been stationed to their designated combat stations.

During the first few days of the war, Egypt used the surprise factor to its full advantage. The Egyptian air force decimated key Israeli bases, command posts, air combat headquarters, missile batteries, and gun emplacements in the Sinai; an estimated 90% of the initially planned targets were hit. The successful air strike was swiftly followed by an equally destructive artillery barrage, and Egyptian troops crossed the Suez Canal and seized the East Bank.[76] Syrian forces also made small advancements in the Golan Heights area, though their success was nowhere near that of the Egyptians in those first few days of the war. Prime Minister Golda Meir later wrote that the early days of the Yom Kippur War were "a near disaster, a nightmare that I experienced and which will always be with me."[77]

---

[75] Anwar Sadat, *In Search of Identity*, trans. Jack L. Rivers (Washington DC: National War College, 1992), 232-233.
[76] Carroll, *Anwar Sadat*, 68.
[77] Ibid., 70.

Golda Meir

Ultimately, the Israeli setback did not last long. Israeli forces countered the Syrians in the Golan Heights, running them out of the area, while Israeli air strikes destroyed Egyptian cities close to the West Bank of the Suez Canal. The resources and foreign aid the two sides had were vastly different; unsurprisingly, the Soviet Union had from the very start of the war no confidence in the Egyptians, calling on Sadat numerous times to negotiate for a ceasefire. On the other hand, the initial victories that Egypt enjoyed and the suddenly real possibility of Israel's defeat spurred the U.S. into action; American tanks and advanced weaponry never before seen in this part of the world were flown in to aid the Israeli forces, and the Israelis were quickly able to overpower the Egyptians. On October 19, nearly two weeks after the surprise attack, Sadat had no choice but to accept a ceasefire.[78] Sadat had never believed that it would be an easy war, but with the U.S. in play, he knew that victory was impossible.

In his autobiography, Sadat called the Yom Kippur War a success, for it had proved that Israel could be attacked and its psyche and pride battered. The victories that Egypt gained, especially at the start of the war, did wonders to restore Arab pride and boost Egyptian morale, as it was Egypt that had destroyed the myth of Israel's invincibility. Over 2,500 Israeli soldiers died in the war (comparable to around 150,000 for a country the size of the U.S.), an estimated $2 billion worth of equipment, weaponry, and infrastructure was destroyed, and the losses to the Israeli economy, due to mobilization and fighting, were estimated at around $7 billion.[79] Additionally, Sadat wrote that the war had significant implications in the diplomatic arena: "Israel began to realize that the temporary possession of our lands did not provide an eternal insurance policy… [and we understood that] no matter how great our military success, war was merely an instrument and not the end in itself. After I saw we had reached our objectives, we limited the suffering and casualties. That also helped us in later diplomatic efforts. A nation cannot bargain when its opponent does not believe it has the power to escalate the stakes if necessary to enforce its will. Paradoxically, I went to war to make peace: until Israel perceived we had sufficient strength to pose a real threat, no peaceful resolution of our conflict was possible."[80]

Shuttle diplomacy led by U.S. Secretary of State Henry Kissinger followed, and agreements were signed in 1974 and 1975 that led to the full disengagement of Egyptian and Israeli troops in the Sinai Peninsula. Still, despite the ceasefire and disengagement agreements, full peace was still far from being achieved. Negotiations staggered and stalled as Israel experienced a government reshuffle, and the U.S.'s own changes in its government – caused by the transition from the Nixon administration to the interim presidency of Gerald Ford – seriously undermined Kissinger's diplomatic efforts.

In 1978, Jimmy Carter was elected president, and Sadat was determined to build a positive and personal relationship with the new leader of the United States. By this time, the Soviet Union had all but cut off its relations with Egypt; for years, the Soviet bloc had assumed that Egypt was in its sphere of influence, but the expulsion of Soviet advisors from Egypt, Sadat's complete disregard for Soviet warnings not to engage Israel in war, and Sadat's newfound friendship with Kissinger and his active involvement in the U.S.-led Egyptian-Israeli peace efforts were the final straws. To the chagrin of many Arab states, Sadat realized that the U.S. was the only country in

---

[78] Ibid., 72.
[79] Ibid., 74.
[80] Sadat, *In Search of Identity*, 238-239.

the world with the resources, power, and influence to guide Israel and Egypt toward full peace. As Sadat later wrote, "He who cannot change the very fabric of his thought will never be able to change reality, and will never, therefore, make any progress."[81]

Sadat and Carter

Among all the dramatic actions Sadat took during his presidency – from his fiery decision to ouster all Soviet advisors from Egypt to his audacious gamble with the Yom Kippur War -- certainly the most dramatic and breathtaking one was his decision to visit Jerusalem. It must be noted that none of Sadat's decisions, including this one, were ever executed on whim or without much thought; Sadat's symbolic visit to Israel – the first visit an Arab leader made to Israeli soil – was calculated and well thought-out. In one simple gesture, Sadat irrevocably changed the nature and tone of the long-running Arab-Israeli conflict, granting Israel the recognition they had been demanding for decades while proving to his newfound ally, the United States, and to the world that Egypt was committed to peace. Against the advice of his aides and the wishes of his fellow Arab heads of state, on November 19, 1977, Sadat landed in Jerusalem.[82]

---

[81] Carroll, *Anwar Sadat*, 81.
[82] Elbendary, "The Long Revolution."

Sadat greets Ezer Weizman, Israeli Defense Minister, in 1978

The following day, on November 20, Sadat headed to the Israeli Knesset to deliver his speech. "I come to you today on solid ground, to shape a new life, to establish peace," he began. The parliamentarians, and much of Israel, were silent as the speech was televised across the country. The words he spoke were unprecedented and had never before been uttered by an Arab leader: "You would like to live with us in this region of the world. In all sincerity, I tell you, we welcome you among us, with full security and safety…today I tell you, and declare it to the whole world, that we accept to live with you in permanent peace based on justice."[83]

When he finished his speech, Sadat was met with thunderous applause both from the Knesset and from the Israeli population. Yitzhak Rabin, who had also personally greeted Sadat at the airport, later wrote: "The mere fact that an Arab leader who had waged war against Israel came forth and stated that he understood our need for security and that a way must be found to meet our legitimate concern was absolutely revolutionary."[84]

When Sadat returned to Cairo, he was welcomed by an electrified population and a parliament that was nearly in full agreement to endorse his actions. Beyond question or doubt, Sadat's visit

---

[83] Transcript of speech taken from: "Egypt-Israel Relations: Address by Egyptian President Anwar Sadat to the Knesset," *Jewish Virtual Library,* accessed August 4, 2014,
https://www.jewishvirtuallibrary.org/jsource/Peace/sadat_speech.html.
[84] Carroll, *Anwar Sadat,* 84.

to Jerusalem was one of the greatest milestones of the twentieth century, becoming a cornerstone in the modern history of the Middle East. But in the months that followed, negotiations with Israel, again facilitated by the U.S., stalled again over the Palestinian issue and territorial disputes. In September 1978, with the hope to finally settle a peace treaty once and for all, President Jimmy Carter invited Sadat and Israeli Prime Minister Begin to Camp David in Washington D.C. For eleven days, the three leaders negotiated, discussed, and argued.

Begin, Carter, and Sadat at Camp David

On September 17, 1978, the two sides were finally able to agree on a framework for peace. In short, the framework stipulated that Israel will execute a full withdrawal from the Sinai Peninsula over a three-year period, while Egypt would develop full peaceful relations with Israel. The fact that there should be transitional agreements established for the West Bank and Gaza, and for continued discussion over the status of Palestinians and Jewish settlers in the occupied territories, was also included.[85] As vague as this framework was, it was an essential step in the peace process, and it ultimately led to the March 1979 signing of the Egyptian-Israeli Peace Treaty.

---

[85] "The Camp David Accords of 1979," BBC News, November 29, 2001,
http://news.bbc.co.uk/2/hi/in_depth/middle_east/israel_and_the_palestinians/key_documents/1632849.stm.

Sadat, Carter, and Begin shake hands at the ceremony announcing the peace agreement

Begin and Sadat appearing before a Joint Session of Congress

To much of Egypt and the world, Sadat was a hero and peacemaker, the epitome of true and willful leadership. Though he experienced great isolation from much of the Arab world after the signing of the treaty with Israel, his people remained his greatest supporters. Sadat quickly turned back to domestic policies, continuing his work with the *infitah* (opening up) of the Egyptian economy and pursuing social and political reforms.

However, during the final months of Sadat's life, internal opposition was beginning to form. Sadat brushed this aside as just another Soviet plot to destabilize this government, but rumors of a plot organized by Egyptian dissidents living abroad to overthrow Sadat emerged. Undeterred, Sadat continued to focus on foreign affairs and the peace effort.[86]

In 1979, the Iranian Revolution swept across the Middle East, the first revolution of its kind to be fueled by a political and radicalized form of Islam. The resulting short-term and long-term effects of the revolution were significant; Islamic fundamentalist and revivalist movements, inspired by the success of the Iranian clerics, began forming and plotting their own revolution in their respective countries, including in Egypt.

On October 6, 1981, Anwar Sadat was assassinated during a victory parade honoring the eighth

---

[86] Pace, "Anwar El-Sadat, the Daring Arab Pioneer of Peace with Israel."

anniversary of the Yom Kippur War. In shocking footage that spread across the world, Sadat and spectators near him were attacked by some of the parade's participants, and as they approached Sadat's position firing weapons, Sadat actually thought it was part of the parade and stood up to salute them. In addition to firing with automatic weapons, grenades were thrown into the crowd as well. Egyptian security forces eventually engaged the assassins and killed and wounded some of them, but Sadat had been mortally wounded in the attack. Hosni Mubarak, who would succeed Sadat and go on to rule Egypt for decades, was also injured in the attack.

A radical militant Islamist group, the Egyptian Islamic Jihad, claimed responsibility, and across the globe, world leaders expressed their dismay, anger, and anguish. Unlike his predecessor Gamal Abdel Nasser's funeral, which was attended by millions, Anwar Sadat was buried in private, surrounded only by his family and close associates, at the Unknown Soldier Memorial in the Nasr City district of Cairo.[87] The inscription on his grave simply reads "Hero of war and peace."[88]

Einsamer Schütze's picture of the tomb of the unknown soldier where Sadat was buried

Chapter 4: The Legacy of Anwar Sadat

When he took office, Sadat was widely regarded as transitional and temporary – a gray interim

---

[87] "Anwar Sadat Killed," *UPI*, 1981, http://www.upi.com/Archives/Audio/Events-of-1981/Anwar-Sadat-Killed.
[88] Mohamed Fadel Fahmy, "30 Years Later, Questions Remain over Sadat Killing, Peace with Israel," *CNN*, October 7, 2011, http://edition.cnn.com/2011/10/06/world/meast/egypt-sadat-assassination/.

figure filling Nasser's shoes until someone with more charisma, energy, and vision could take over. He was mocked as "Nasser's poodle," his peasant origins were ridiculed, and he was criticized as one without his own vision and goals. Indeed, not many knew how deeply he had affected Nasser and his presidency, how great of a role he played in the 1952 revolution, and how determined he was to take and keep the presidency he had inherited. Though his start was rocky, Sadat would become one of the most imaginative, visionary, and daring leaders of the century.

Perhaps what made Sadat into such a catalytic force in regional and global politics was his ability to think beyond the established norm and traditions. Sadat wrote in his autobiography about the long-held enmity Arabs have held against Israel, and the strict taboo of even hinting at any kind of support for or rapprochement with the Israelis. He recalled how Prime Begin, and many other Israeli leaders before him, had challenged Arab leaders to come to Israel and meet face-to-face to discuss the problems rather than shouting insults across the thousands of miles that separated the two countries. "We were calling for our land, but we were refusing to ask it of those who occupied it. We were calling for our rights, but we were refusing to sit down with those who had deprived us of them," Sadat wrote in his autobiography. "All we did – what the Arabs still do, even now – was to sit in our capitals and issue warnings to Israel and her friends."[89] And Sadat was determined to set himself apart from the others, to write history.

Thus, unlike so many of his fellow Arab leaders, Sadat was willing to think past illogical contempt and long-held political taboos. He was daring, courageous, and determined enough to do the unthinkable to get the job done. And indeed, that was what he did; he extended the hand of peace to a long-time foe, reversing Egypt's longstanding policy and proclaiming his willingness to recognize Israel as a sovereign state.

Although he will always be remembered for his courage and boldness, for his significant role in global diplomacy, and his hard-earned achievements in the peace process, Anwar Sadat's ultimate legacy remains uncertain, even today. The negotiations that were begun by Sadat have achieved neither a resolution nor an amelioration of the Arab-Israeli conflict. He left behind a tense and difficult relationship, in which he himself was a key part that held it together. So strongly had Sadat fought for peace that he began to personify it; upon Sadat's death, the Israelis' confidence in continued efforts for peace with his successor Hosni Mubarak dwindled. Campaigns emerged in Israel to block the withdrawal process from the Sinai – a key component of the 1979 peace treaty. As Israeli Interior Minister Yosef Burg put it aptly, "We shall find out if a man or an idea was killed."[90]

Sadat also left behind an isolated Egypt – an outcast among its fellow Arab states. The treaty with Israel had been costly; Egypt was suspended from the Arab League in 1979, and political

---

[89] El-Sadat, *Those I Have Known*, 102-103.
[90] Carroll, *Anwar Sadat*, 104.

alliances realigned and shifted against Egyptian interests.[91] It would be years before the Arab League would lift the suspension, and Egypt can return to its position as the dominant player in the region.

Anwar Sadat nonetheless taught the world important lessons. He was a man who never feared to self-examine his qualities and reexamine his goals and intentions; thus, he taught the importance of altering ingrained habits and long-held ways of thinking – some formed by one's own self, and some shaped by history, society, and culture – especially when these old mindsets have proved to be ineffective, harmful, or unable to fit into the reality of the world. He taught the importance of taking risks, even when operating at the highest level of governance, for the furthering of peace.

Finally, Anwar Sadat's focus on the big picture – on always being able to know where he and his country were in the overall scheme of things, on where they were going and how – was an essential component of his presidency, and later his legacy. Sadat's dislike for being bogged down by details was well documented; a declassified U.S. government report on the personality profiles of Begin and Sadat, put together in preparation for the Camp David Accords, noted "preoccupation with the big picture" and "abhorrence of details" as key elements of Sadat's personality.[92] Furthermore, his daughter, Camelia Anwar Sadat, has written that her father once told her that she must always walk with her head held high, for then she would be able to "see problems as the small matters that they are. If details do not deserve attention, do not give them attention…Envision things and calculate them….understand a goal and then plan how to reach it."[93]

Indeed, Anwar Sadat was a visionary, too curious to maintain the status quo, too bold to be afraid of risks. Though his legacy has and will continue to be debated, and though the true and full peace between Israelis and Arabs that Sadat envisioned has yet to be achieved, he remains one of the greatest and most courageous leaders in the history of the Middle East.

---

[91] John Kifner, "Confrontation in the Gulf; Badly Divided Arab League Votes to Return Headquarters to Cairo," *The New York Times*, September 11, 1990, http://www.nytimes.com/1990/09/11/world/confrontation-gulf-badly-divided-arab-league-votes-return-headquarters-cairo.html.

[92] Jerrold Post, "Personality Profiles in Support of the Camp David Summit," *Studies in Intelligence* (Spring 1979): 3.

[93] Sadat and El-Sayed, "Anwar Sadat and His Vision," 4.

Bibliography

Alagna, Magdalena. *Anwar Sadat*. New York: Rosen Publishing Group, 2004.

Alterman, Jon B. "Introduction." In *Sadat and His Legacy*, edited by Jon B. Alterman,, vii-xx. Washington DC: Washington Institute for Near East Policy, 1998.

"Anwar Al-Sadat." Accessed June 2, 2014. https://web.archive.org/web/20090125000520/http://ibiblio.org/sullivan/bios/Sadat-bio.html.

"Anwar Sadat Killed." *UPI*. 1981. http://www.upi.com/Archives/Audio/Events-of-1981/Anwar-Sadat-Killed.

Butt, Gerald. "Lesson From History: 1955 Baghdad Pact." *BBC News*. February 26, 2003. http://news.bbc.co.uk/2/hi/middle_east/2801487.stm.

Carroll, Raymond. *Anwar Sadat*. New York: F. Watts, 1982.

"Egypt-Israel Relations: Address by Egyptian President Anwar Sadat to the Knesset." *Jewish Virtual Library*. Accessed August 4, 2014. https://www.jewishvirtuallibrary.org/jsource/Peace/sadat_speech.html.

Elbendary, Amina. "The Long Revolution." *Al-Ahram*. July 18, 2002. http://weekly.ahram.org.eg/2002/595/sc2.htm.

El-Sadat, Anwar. *Those I Have Known*. New York: Continuum, 1984.

Fahmy, Mohamed Fadel. "30 Years Later, Questions Remain over Sadat Killing, Peace with Israel." *CNN*. October 7, 2011. http://edition.cnn.com/2011/10/06/world/meast/egypt-sadat-assassination/.

Finklestone, Joseph. *Anwar Sadat: Visionary Who Dared*. London: Frank Cass Publishers, 1996.

Gawrych, George W. *The 1973 Arab-Israeli War: The Albatross of Decisive Victory*. Combat Studies Institute, U.S. Army Command and General Staff College, 1996.

Gordon, Joel. *Nasser's Blessed Movement: Egypt's Free Officers and the July Revolution*. New York: Oxford University Press, 1992.

Khalid, Sunni M. "The Root: Race and Racism Divide Egypt." *NPR*. February 7, 2011. http://www.npr.org/2011/02/07/133562448/the-root-egypts-race-problem.

Kifner, John. "Confrontation in the Gulf; Badly Divided Arab League Votes to Return Headquarters to Cairo." *The New York Times.* September 11, 1990. http://www.nytimes.com/1990/09/11/world/confrontation-gulf-badly-divided-arab-league-votes-return-headquarters-cairo.html.

Metz, Helen Chapin. Ed. *Egypt: A Country Study*. Washington: GPO for the Library of Congress, 1990.

Morris, Benny. *Righteous Victims: A History of the Zionist-Arab Conflict, 1881-1998.* New York: Vintage Books, 1999.

Pace, Eric. "Anwar El-Sadat, the Daring Arab Pioneer of Peace with Israel." *The New York Times.* October 7, 1981. http://www.nytimes.com/learning/general/onthisday/bday/1225.html.

Podeh, Elie and Onn Winckler. "Introduction: Nasserism as a Form of Populism." In *Rethinking Nasserism: Revolution and Historical Memory in Modern* Egypt, edited by Elie Podeh and Onn Winckler, 10-42. Gainesville, FL: University Press of Florida, 2004.

Post, Jerrold. "Personality Profiles in Support of the Camp David Summit." *Studies in Intelligence* (Spring 1979): 1-5.

"Mohamed Anwar El-Sadat." *State Information Service Your Gateway to Egypt.* July 20, 2009. http://www.sis.gov.eg/En/Templates/Articles/tmpArticles.aspx?ArtID=1665#.U921uvmSy18.

Rabinovich, Abraham. *The Yom Kippur War: The Epic Encounter that Transformed the Middle East*. New York: Schocken Books, 2004.

Sadat, Anwar. *In Search of Identity*. Translated by Jack L. Rivers. Washington DC: National War College, 1992.

Sadat, Camelia Anwar and Ahmed Maher El-Sayed. "Anwar Sadat and His Vision." In *Sadat and His Legacy*, edited by Jon B. Alterman, 1-10. Washington DC: Washington Institute for Near East Policy, 1998.

Sullivan, George. *Sadat: The Man Who Changed Mid-East History.* New York: Walker, 1981.

"The Camp David Accords of 1979." *BBC News.* November 29, 2001. http://news.bbc.co.uk/2/hi/in_depth/middle_east/israel_and_the_palestinians/key_documents/1632849.stm.

Vanetik, Boaz and Zaki Shalom. "The White House Middle East Policy in 1973 as a Catalyst for the Outbreak of the Yom Kippur War." *Israeli Studies* 16, no. 1 (2011): 53-78.

Wagner, Heather Lehr. *Anwar Sadat and Menachem Begin: Negotiating Peace in the Middle East.* New York: Infobase Publishing, 2007.

Printed in Great Britain
by Amazon